STERLING B. FREEMAN

Author & Illustrator

PUBLISHED BY PASSION-POWERED PUBLISHING
PO Box 340625, Tampa, FL 33694

Cover Design and Illustrations 2019 by Sterling B. Freeman
Illustrations' Line Art and Colored by Bilal Karaca

Website: LittleLightSeries.com
ISBN: 978-0-578-62894-3

Once upon a time,
on a night with a moon,
sat a boy with his toy
alone in his room.

Just a little red car and

the vroom of his voice

as the sound of his engine that made too

much noise.

So, up came mother
in her robe that was red
to see what was the matter
and poke in her head.
When she saw that her son
was still up playing,
she said, "Little boy, it is late.
You should be in bed."

"But, mother, you don't understand,"
with a voice like a weep.
"I've been at it all night.
Closed my eyes will not keep.
I toss and I turn but still not one peep.
No matter how hard I try,
I just can't go to sleep."

"Oh, nonsense, my son,"
the mother said with a wink.
"First, I'll go down and get you
something to drink."

With a warm glass of milk,
she was back in a blink.
With a grin on her face:
"I've got just the thing."

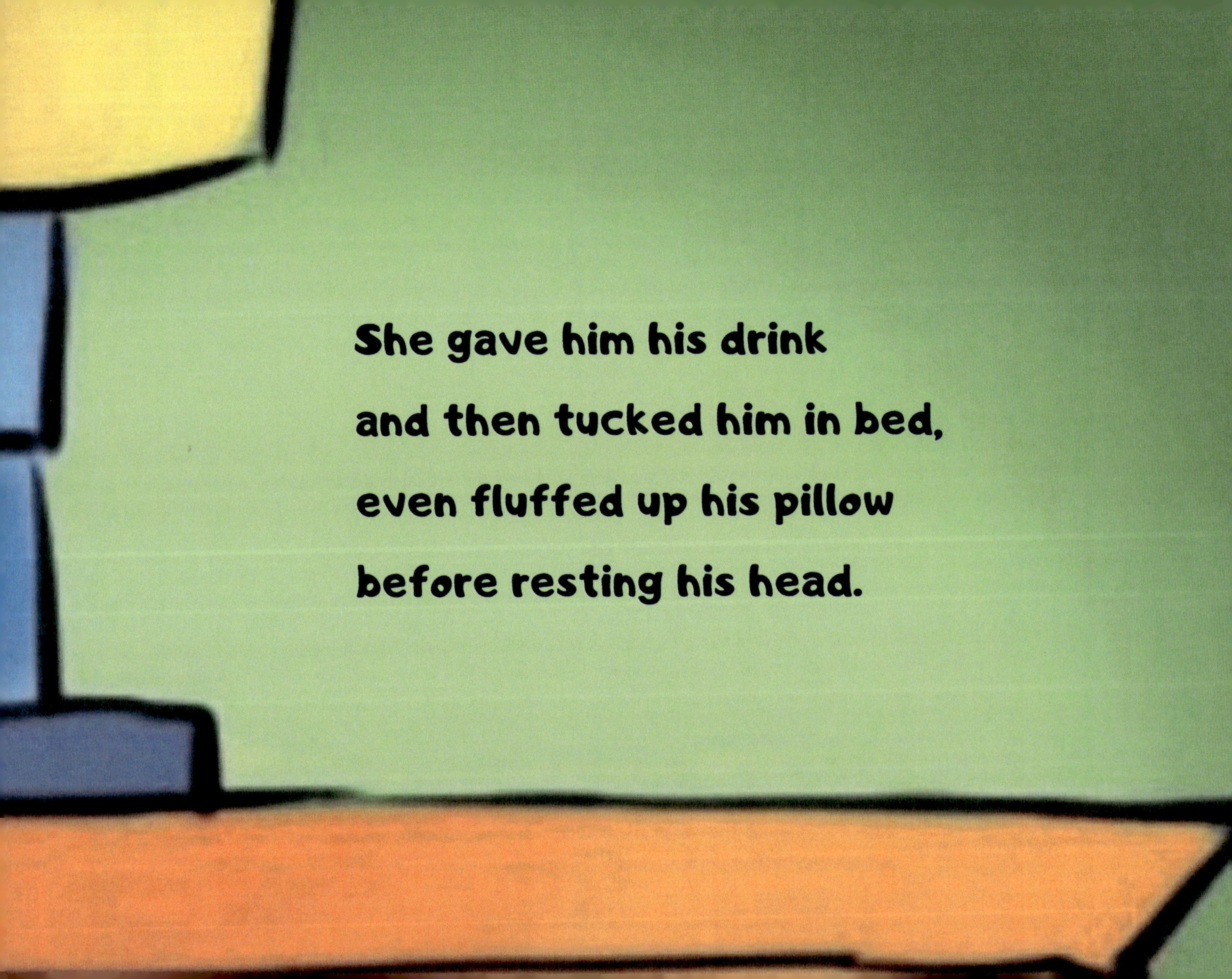

She gave him his drink
and then tucked him in bed,
even fluffed up his pillow
before resting his head.

"When I was your age,
and I couldn't sleep,
you know what I'd do?
Count sheep."

With the squint of his eyes
and a look of doubt,
quite puzzled, the boy
started looking about.
To his left and his right,
he couldn't figure it out.
"What do you mean, mother?
There are none to count."

"Oh, no no, silly.
You make them up in your mind,
jumping over a fence
one sheep at a time."

"But how many, mother?
What color? What kind?"
"Shhh, little one.
No more questions. Just try."

SKATER SHEEP
???

The boy finished his milk.
Gave the mustache a wipe.
Putting the little red car
on the nightstand to the right.
Mother leaned in and kissed
his forehead goodnight.
And, before leaving the room,
she turned out the light.

So, once again all alone in his room,

the boy started to count: 1, 2,

SKATER SHEEP
#2

3, 4, 5, then...Zzzz zzzzz zzz.

Out just like his light.

LET THE DREAMING BEGIN.

Made in the USA
Middletown, DE
19 August 2022